Elders Today

Opportunities of a Lifetime

Text and Photographs
Nader Robert Shabahangi

Founding Publisher: Nader R. Shabahangi, Ph.D.
Managing Publisher: Nader R. Shabahangi, Ph.D.
Photos courtesy of Nader Shabahangi. Cover photo of Rhoda Curtis by Nader Shabahangi.

Elders Academy Press' publications are available through most bookstores. Substantial discounts on bulk quantities are available to corporations, professional associations, and other organizations. Email books@pacificinstitute.org for details and discount information.

Elders Today: Opportunities of a Lifetime is sponsored by Pacific Institute, its eldercare program AgeSong Institute, and the AgeSong Elder Communities. This book is published by Elders Academy Press, a program of Pacific Institute.

ISBN 978-0-9847097-0-0 (Soft Cover)
Library of Congress Cataloging-in-Publication Data
Shabahangi, Nader.
Elders Today: Opportunities of a Lifetime/Nader Shabahangi.—1st ed.
Includes bibliographical references.
ISBN 978-0-9847097-0-0
1. Elders—Eldership 2. Older People—Poetry. 3. Aging—Poetry. 4. Alzheimer's disease—Patients—Care. 1. Shabahangi, Nader Robert, 1957-. II. Title.
2011940724

"The faces in *Elders Today* tell the stories of lives lived, laughter and tears, and the wisdom and compassion that develops as we grow older. They show all of us that independent of our age and health, our hearts and souls are present, communicating with those around us, creating community. These photographs will not only make you see but also feel the beauty and depth of our elders."

— Max Schupbach, Ph.D.
International Consultant, Founder of the Deep Democracy Institute

"*Elders Today* is an amazingly open and brilliant view of older people. Dr. Shabahangi's wonderful writing and photographs reveal new vistas of aging that include joy and suffering, loss and depths of presence. In this new book, we not only learn to appreciate what it means to be an elder; we can't help but actually look forward to becoming elders ourselves."

— Arny and Amy Mindell, Ph.D.
Authors and Founder of Process Oriented Psychology

"As the first of an unprecedented number of Baby Boomers reaches age sixty-five, they are entering what Dr. William Thomas calls a *second crucible* as they begin to navigate the transition to elderhood. Will this hugely influential generation transform our view of aging, and what will be their guide? Dr. Nader Shabahangi offers us a vision for the second half of life, not as a slow decline toward death but as a kind of ripening–synthesizing one's experience and perspective into wisdom and creating a legacy for future generations. This small but important book weds powerful words and images to create a compelling and challenging road map for age—a destination where even those who live with significant forgetfulness can endow us with the gifts of their presence and insight. Your future begins here."

— G. Allen Power, M.D., FACP
Geriatrician, Eden Mentor, and author of Dementia Beyond Drugs

There are young people who are old, there are old people who are young. If you carry in you this flame of progress and transformation, if you are ready to leave everything behind so that you may advance with an alert step, if you are always open to a new progress, a new improvement, a new transformation, then you are eternally young.

Everything that has been done is always nothing compared with what remains to be done. Do not look behind. Look ahead, always ahead and go forward always.

—Sri Aurobindo
Ashram, 2004

Dedication

To the elders in the world whose care,
heart, and wisdom instill our lives with
love, beauty and hope.

And to my friend Thomas who,
foregoing his second half of life, left us
too soon – we miss you.

Table of Contents

The first half of life just sets the stage —
the second half provides life's real opportunities.

Our modern civilization is so obsessed with youth that almost no one today understands the significance of growing older. I want to tell everyone that the first half of life just sets the stage. That is when we make mistakes and explore what the world has to offer. It is in the second half, with family and career behind us, that we have the experience to know life's real opportunities and the opportunity and resources to give back to life and pursue Self-realization.

And I am going to tell every older person in this country, and demonstrate it with my life: "You can improve your performance in the second part of life. You can enrich precious qualities of which you had only a faint inkling when you were younger. You can take up a new career of service, even if you are in a wheelchair." That's what life is for. I may not be able to play soccer or swim... , but I live a million times better than I did when I was in my twenties, and my life is a million times more significant.

— Sri Eknath Easwaran,
With My Love and Blessings

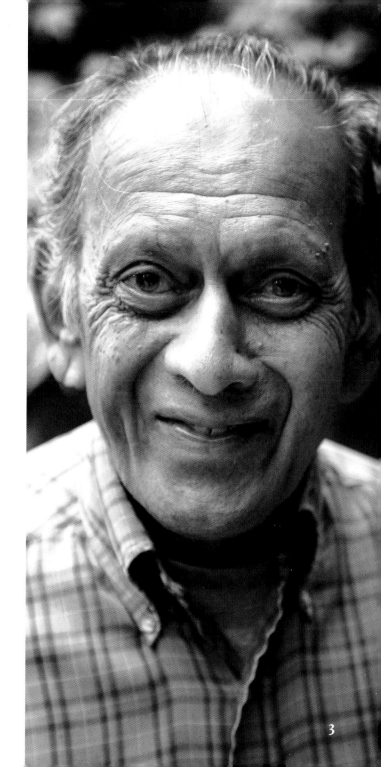

What we need is a radical reinterpretation of longevity that makes elders (and their needs) central to our collective pursuit of happiness and well-being.

— Dr. William Thomas
Geriatrician & Founder of the Eden Alternative

Foreword

Growing old is full of the same anxieties that beset us when we enter puberty. It is full of surprises.

What's the matter with me?
Where are my feet?
Nobody pays attention to me; it's as if I am invisible.
People look past me.
Nobody understands me.

There's no way to escape these anxieties, or to pretend they don't exist. What we need to do is to accept the limitations of who we are and what we are, and then to reach beyond those boundaries. Our cultures, whatever they are, and from whatever origins, impose upon us expectations as we grow up and age, and we internalize these expectations. Unfortunately, by accepting others' definitions of who we are and how we are supposed to behave, we limit our own possibilities. It takes insight and courage to move beyond those limitations.

We have to take deep breaths and decide to move beyond the boundaries others have decreed for us. When our hips ache, we can try a slow exercise. If we feel useless, we can take ourselves out of our paralysis and take action, any action – sign a petition, join a virtual march, write letters to the editor and/or Congress. If we feel sleepy, we can take a nap without feeling guilty. We usually don't have nine-to-five jobs that demand twenty-four/seven attention. We can relax!

Young people will understand and appreciate us more if we reach out to them. We need to ask for help when we need it. I reach for a stranger's arm if I need to cross a street; if I'm walking on a narrow path, I ask for help. Most people are surprised and flattered.

My message to all of us – and the message of this book – is to look at our aging as an opportunity for growing, learning, and ongoing creative expressions. We no longer need to feel that we have to live up to anyone else's expectations except our own. The following pages allow you to reflect deeply on what aging has to offer – freedom and liberation that no other phase of life provides.

— Rhoda Curtis, 93 ¾ years mature;
author of *Rhoda: Her First Ninety Years* and
After Ninety, What;
monthly contributor to the *Huffington Post*.

Introduction

Perhaps more important than the content of this book itself is the fact that it needs to be written. One can theorize much about why we live in an era where we would need to emphasize that elders and what they offer us belong to one of the most beautiful expressions of human existence. This small book cannot and does not want to address this curious circumstance. Rather, it would like to bring awareness to the all too obvious fact that a human life is a complex and rich process of becoming, of continued growth and development. As such, human beings possess the opportunity to

7

mature and deepen with time. The term *elder* is used here as a term of respect for just this maturity, often gained only through a lifetime of experience and learning. We frequently refer to humans who are elders as wise. Wisdom is not easy to define and is somewhat akin to our understanding of time: we know what it is and what it feels like until we are asked to explain it. Perhaps we can approach an understanding of what we mean by wisdom through what it feels like to us. Words such as unhurried, measured, restrained, patient, reasonable, kind, empathic, dignified, aware, careful, and considerate come to mind. Almost all of us would agree that these are desirable qualities of human mind and behavior. Yet, when I asked a group of elders in a recent gathering what they thought old age had given them in terms of learning, many were reluctant to value the above given list of adjectives as important expressions of their growth.

This ought not to surprise given we live in a culture which only tangentially values these qualities, as if they are nice to have but are not really that important for getting on with our real lives. A review of the curricula at our schools and universities will attest to this fact. So, it is left to all of us, young and old, to be proponents of these values and help re-instill them into our everyday culture and society. These values are increasingly needed to counter the tendency of an ever quickening pace in our lives and where decision-making is based more on short-term than long-term ends.

Another reason is the present-day tendency to regard the material dimension of our existence, of having and doing, as more central than our subjective, being and relational aspects of life. The quality of being refers here to who we are from a feeling perspective, and to our enduring values. Having and doing, in contrast, refer to our material dimension, to our outward accomplishments. Elders can show us to be more balanced in this regard, valuing both the material achievements and security while emphasizing the importance of relationship, of feeling content and at peace with oneself and others. By providing us with the long view,

elders remind us through their very presence that we all move towards the end of our lives, irrespective of our speed and achievement.

In this regard, elders remind us of the big questions of life: what really matters to me? What gives me a true sense of contentment, of feeling useful inside? What are the moments I cherish and how do I remember those as guideposts for living my life? How do my actions, thoughts and behaviors further who I would like to become? What is the vision I have of myself, of the society within which I live, to which I would like to contribute? What are the values I hold dear and for which I want to stand? What would I like to leave behind when I part from this world? These questions are central, I believe, to living a life that is worth living. It is in joining with the elders of today that each one of us can be enriched and deepened, that our culture and societies can be reminded of what makes us essentially human.

— Nader R. Shabahangi
San Francisco, October 2011

Treat an Elder today the same way you want to be treated when you are old.

Many of us are afraid of growing old.

We think that aging means that our bodies will become progressively weaker and that we will no longer fit the idealized image of youth. We forget that with the passing of years our life experiences increase, our knowledge deepens, and our souls mature.

Societies once honored elders with respect and regard. Today, more than ever, society needs the wisdom and caring that comes with age.

Remember the words of Oriah Mountain Dreamer:

"It doesn't interest me how old you are. I want to know if you will risk looking like a fool for love, for your dreams, for the adventure of being alive."

When you help an Elder, you also help the part of yourself growing old.

Young and Old

Perhaps elders move slower, but they know where they are going.

Perhaps elders take longer to decide, but their decisions feel wiser.

Perhaps they think less quickly, but their thoughts are more insightful.

Perhaps their eyesight is not as sharp, but their vision is more profound.

Perhaps their hearing has lessened, but they know what is worth listening to.

Perhaps they struggle with modern technology, but they understand more about the mystery of life.

Another View

Elders are an enormous untapped source of experience, time, and wisdom.

The motivation and ability to learn do not belong to the young only – learning continues throughout our lives.

Happiness and joy, above all, are attitudes towards life, unrelated to our age.

Elders communicate their challenges and needs in many different ways.

Making wise decisions is not the same as rapid-information processing.

Where is the wisdom
we have lost in knowledge?
Where is the knowledge
we have lost in information?
— *T.S. Eliot*

Caring Support – a Gift of our Elders

In our busy lives and struggles we often lose the value of caring support as a basic expression of our humanity. This value shows itself especially in our attitude to elders today. We often witness that care has turned into a routine or mechanical act. Care is understood more as a burden, something to be done that takes our time away from something more important. Imagine if we could shift our attitude to care, if we could understand it as the very essence of our lives.

Specifically, this would mean that

- the person for whom you care is your emotional and spiritual teacher;
- our emotional, physical and spiritual well-being are inseperable and ought to be sustained as a whole;
- through our concern we remember that our deepest need is as much to give as to receive supportive care;
- in caring for others we experience our relatedness to *Being*.

In being with elders, we can learn the art of communication. They teach us that communication is much more than just verbal language and happens on many different levels, often non-verbal. In being with elders we learn, often in subtle ways, that

- when elders talk gently, we learn to communicate more slowly;
- when elders attend to our presence, we learn to be more present to ourselves;
- when elders listen to us, we learn the value of listening;
- when elders are patient with us, we learn patience in return;
- when elders wish to know us, we develop the courage to know ourselves and others;
- when elders place their trust in us, we learn to believe in ourselves.

The Human at Play

Many elders, especially if forgetful, are spontaneous and playful. Human beings connect with their true essence when at play. In play we

- feel removed from intellectual and worldly restrictions;
- are in the flow of the moment, free from limitations and our controlling mind;
- give up our desire to achieve or produce;
- stop judging others and ourselves;
- are with all that expresses itself at any given moment;
- see the world with new eyes that do not marginalize, or label the world into categories of good and bad.

Our attachment to memory can limit our ability to play and be truly in the moment. In the words of George Bernard Shaw: *We don't stop playing because we grow old. We grow old because we stop playing.*

Living in the Question

Living in the question means to appreciate the mystery that envelops us. Our sense that we can control and direct our lives is only one possible truth. There's another possible truth, perhaps even more powerful:

- this truth places our direction as much in the hands of some other force – whether it is called God, Nature, Tao, or Quantum Mind – than in our own hands;
- views events and relationships as meaningful because we cannot help but to ascribe meaning to them;
- understands these events and experiences as part of our life-path, our destiny.

The basic assumption here is that life is purposeful, that somehow all – people, planet, universe – has meaning.

Expanding our Awareness

Each difference we encounter in others affords us the opportunity to learn acceptance and patience within ourselves; it also enlarges our perception of the world. We understand more fully that often

- our mainstream culture does not allow much room for variability in personality;
- we are expected to stay within a range of familiar behaviors and communication styles;

- our attachment to *normality* makes it difficult for us to appreciate elders and all they offer us.

How we look at elders from our younger point of view is also how we look at our own aging.

- If we judge elders for being slow, we might judge ourselves for not being quick enough;

- If we look at elders as less attractive, we might be critical of our own appearance;
- If we see elders as being disconnected from present-day society, we might have removed ourselves from the deep source of life.

We humans appreciate constancy and predictability over change and unpredictability – but change is the only constant as we continue to live and age. The more we learn to be with change, the more we are with the flow of life. And the more we are accepting of the vicissitudes of life, the more we stand in awe of our amazing existence in this world.

It is miraculous to be alive, to be driven to deepen who we are, driven to continually grow and mature.

The Uses of Not

Thirty spokes
Meet in a hub.
Where the wheel isn't
Is where it is useful.

Hollowed out,
Clay makes a pot.
Where the pot is not
Is where it is useful.

Cut doors and windows
To make a room.
Where the room isn't,
There is room for you.

So the profit in what is
Is in the use of what
Isn't.

—Lao Tzu
Tao Te Ching
(translation by Ursula K. LeGuin)

Beyond Good and Bad

For many of us, Alzheimer's disease and other forms of dementia are a source of fear. We think that a meaningful life is only possible with memory and cognitive abilities. This viewpoint disparages the millions of Americans and countless others around the world who are forgetful in one way or another – and all of us are, really.

Our current attitude about remembering and forgetting mirrors our dominant dualistic thinking. This thinking asks questions such as

- What is right and what is wrong?
- What is acceptable and unacceptable?
- What is healthy and what is pathological?

Such thinking

- regards remembering as preferable to forgetting and pathologizes forgetting as dementia;
- describes memory-loss as cognitive impairment.

However, such dualistic thinking is a story interchangeable with another point of view and story.

A Different Story

We can understand forgetfulness – what the medical community calls dementia – as having purpose and meaning, not as simply a disease.

This means that we can see

- people with forgetfulness as teaching us profound lessons about life and living;
- people with forgetfulness as offering us an opportunity to become more insightful and aware, thus allowing us to enter deeper into our souls.

This different story

- understands forgetting as an important gift that allows for something else to emerge;
- describes an attitude that looks for meaning and purpose behind symptoms and conditions that appear before us.

In this story we emphasize

- that humans inhabit a meaningful universe where life is not accidental, and events and conditions are not pathological;
- that we can never understand the essence of all there is in the world, but can only point to it;
- that life will always remain enigmatic and mysterious.

This new and different story requires a shift in attitude, that is

- a fundamental change in the way we view the world and ourselves;
- a curiosity and an openness to all that is;
- an attitude of *not-knowing*, allowing what manifests itself to present itself in the way it actually *is*, not in the way we think we know it.

The Many Gifts of Forgetting

Forgetting allows us to be present with what manifests itself to us at this moment.

- Instead of drifting minds, forgetting can allow us to be here now;
- Instead of being speedy, even frantic, forgetting can allow us to be still;
- Instead of feeling burdened by the everyday, forgetting can allow us to be less preoccupied with agendas, preconceptions, and goals.

Nietzsche
On Forgetting
and Happiness

"But in the case of the smallest and the greatest happiness, it is always just one thing alone that makes happiness happiness: the ability to forget, or, expressed in more scholarly fashion, the capacity to feel ahistorically over the entire course of its duration. Anyone who cannot forget the past entirely and set himself down on the threshold of the moment, anyone who cannot stand, without dizziness or fear, on one single point like a victory goddess, will never know what happiness is; worse, he will never do anything that makes others happy."

— Friedrich Nietzsche
Unfashionable Observations

Learning from Elders

In our experience of being with elders, we have learned

- to be present and focused on the other;
- to appreciate the importance of being in the moment and to understand that past and future are contained therein;
- to value equally joy and laughter, pain and suffering, confusion and clarity;
- to let go of preconceptions and ideas of how the world and reality ought to be;
- to challenge our ideas of what constitutes achievement and productivity;
- to keep questioning what truly is important in our lives.

Elders, in the way they live and the way they are, model for us a very different approach to life and being. This approach provides us with a much needed expansion to our present way of life.

Elders teach us about

- expanding our perception and awareness of reality;
- our attachments to what we know, to what we like and dislike;
- going slow and focusing on the now;
- the many important non-verbal ways of communication;
- how much we are caught up in everyday details that rarely give us the feeling of meaningfulness and true encounter with the world;
- what makes us human.

Old Age as Opportunity for Inner Growth

May I suggest that human beings' potential for change and growth is much greater than we are willing to admit and that old age be regarded not as the age of stagnation but as the age of opportunities for inner growth? Old people must not be treated as patients, nor regard their retirement as a prolonged state of resignation.

The years of old age may enable us to attain the high values we failed to sense, the insights we have missed, the wisdom we ignored. They are indeed formative years, rich in possibilities to unlearn the follies of a lifetime, to see through inbred self-deceptions, to deepen understanding and compassion, to widen the horizon of honesty, to refine the sense of fairness.

One ought to enter old age the way one enters the senior year at a university, in exciting anticipation of consummation. Rich in perspective, experienced in failure, people advanced in years are capable of shedding prejudices and the fever of vested interests. They do not see in every fellow human a person who stands in their way, and competitiveness may cease to be their way of thinking.

We must seek ways to overcome the traumatic fear of being old, the prejudice, the discrimination against those advanced in years. All human beings are created equal, including those advanced in years. Being old is not necessarily the same as being stale. The effort to restore the dignity of old age will depend on our ability to revive the equation of old age and wisdom. Wisdom is the substance upon which the inner security of the old will forever depend. But the attainment of wisdom is the work of a life time.

— Abraham Joshua Heschel (1961)

Warning

When I am an old woman I shall wear purple
With a red hat which doesn't go, and doesn't suit me.
And I shall spend my pension on brandy and summer gloves
And satin sandals, and say we've no money for butter.
I shall sit down on the pavement when I'm tired
And gobble up samples in shops and press alarm bells
And run my stick along the public railings
And make up for the sobriety of my youth.
I shall go out in my slippers in the rain
And pick flowers in other people's gardens
And learn to spit.

You can wear terrible shirts and grow more fat
And eat three pounds of sausages at a go
Or only bread and pickles for a week
And hoard pens and pencils and beermats and things in boxes.

But now we must have clothes that keep us dry
And pay our rent and not swear in the street
And set a good example for the children.
We must have friends to dinner and read the papers.

But maybe I ought to practice a little now?
So people who know me are not too shocked and surprised
When suddenly I am old, and start to wear purple.

— Jenny Joseph

The Long View

Elders have developed the keen ability to see the long view of life. Through all the years of experience, through the many trials, joys and tribulations, elders have understood about the ebb and flow, and that any change takes time. Elders have thus developed a sense of equanimity and patience.

Through their long view of life, elders understand about the limits of knowledge, its cyclical nature. They understand that knowledge is more often than not rooted in social and cultural mores and an individual's feelings and perceptions. This awareness brings forth an appreciation of how much is unknown, may never be known. It gives rise to what we call awe – a stance towards the world filled with amazement about the nature of this world and everything that exists.

An attitude of awe looks at the world and existence with a deep sense of gratitude and acceptance. It understands that life is not about the things themselves but about how we see them, about our attitude towards what is present in front of us. Such an attitude appreciates that life is filled with mysteries, and is itself a mystery.

Lao Tzu, a few thousand years ago, expressed this long view as follows:

You don't have to go out the door
To know what goes on in the world.
You don't have to look out the window
To see the way of heaven.
The farther you go,
The less you know.

So the wise soul
Doesn't go, but knows;
Doesn't look, but sees;
Doesn't do, but gets it done.

—Lao Tzu
Tao Te Ching
(translation by Ursula K. LeGuin)

Wise elders have a sense of what wants and needs to happen, not because of their own wishes and desires, but because they are in tune with the larger process, whatever its name might be.

By being in tune with this process, doing becomes not-doing, doing becomes effortless. This is what Lao Tzu means when he writes that the wise soul doesn't do, but gets it done.

Being connected with the process helps to slow us down. This permits us to notice the often subtle communication within and without that allows us to be in tune with the world and ourselves.

Slowing down is an important step to becoming still. Being still helps our openness to listening. Elders today are the wise souls we need to learn how to live deep and meaningful lives in harmony with the world.

Re-Visioning Life

"**Y**es – the springtimes needed you. Often a star was waiting for you to notice it. A wave rolled toward you out of the distant past, or as you walked under an open window, a violin yielded itself to your hearing."

— Rainer Maria Rilke
Duino Elegies

Spring, that beautiful, wondrous time of year when all life emerges from its long wintery sleep, needs us humans to appreciate its beauty. We have been accustomed to thinking of the world as outside of us. When Rilke reminds us that Spring needs us, desires our seeing, feeling, hearing and touching, we might be taken aback at first – how is it that the world

needs us? That a distant star longs to be noticed by us? Can we revision living in a world that is inextricably part of us and we are part of it? Heidegger emphasizes this point when he renames humans *beings-in-the-world* – an expression that underlines that people and world are always already together, cannot be separated. Such an attitude understands the divine in everyone and everything, around and in us. Categories such as outer and inner,

you and me, lose their meaning. Many mystics present us with such a vision, one of those Rumi: "Out beyond ideas of right-doing and wrong-doing there is a field. I'll meet you there."

Recent imaginative thinkers and writers have called this field the Processmind, Quantum Field, or Collective Unconscious. In this field, categories cease to exist. *Hen kai pan*, the Hellenic Greeks used to shout: One in All, All in One.

Perhaps it is time, as the wise have told us throughout the ages, to remember our connectedness to the All, to deeply feel how the world needs us to be more of an elder, to be more gentle and kind, more grateful and aware.

In small ways only are we in control of our lives. This understanding can fill with us with a sense of humility towards life. Elders today can teach us this humility, can urge us to reflect on the nature of our own existence.

As with life itself, the beginning needs the end, the end the beginning. The first half of life needs the second half, the second the first. We complete the last stanza of our poem of life at the moment we transition to whatever lies next.

We do not stop being creative as we enter old age. On the contrary, something about us, call it human spirit or essence, pushes us to be the immensely curious beings we are, continually in search of what lies next – until our very last breath and, perhaps, beyond. ∎

The invariable mark
of wisdom is to see
the miraculous in
the common.
— Ralph W. Emerson

Acknowledgment

I am grateful to many friends and colleagues who have helped me with this book. Specifically, the elders living at the AgeSong Elder Communities have taught me so much about living life with a different focus and depth.

I am particularly thankful to Pat Fox and John Bailes who made important suggestions and changes to the text. I am grateful to Finley Kipp for her patience and great skill in graphic design, and to Troy Piwowarski for his editorial help and precision.

I owe my gratitude to the staff of AgeSong and to Pacific Institute students, interns, volunteers, supervisors and directors – they all contributed in many different ways to this book.

This work stands firmly on the shoulders of mentor and friend Max Schupbach whose continuous guidance and support of the eldership vision outlined here is truly inspirational. And I am deeply indebted to Arny and Amy Mindell, to their brilliant and tireless efforts of understanding and deepening human consciousness and awareness.

To the Board of Pacific Institute I owe my gratitude for supporting the AgeSong vision as I do to the leadership and care-partner team of the AgeSong Elder Communities.

I am grateful to my partner Ladan who stands by me throughout this journey called 'life' – her love and support are part of the many miracles I am blessed to experience.

To my mother and grandparents I owe the love I have for elders and growing old – they have shown me the beauty of age and old age, to love and care for all that is. Their spirit continues to live in all I am and do every day.

References

The following bibliography constitutes the sources and much of the backdrop and inspiration for this book. This literature also serves as a way to move from the causal and literal mind-set to one more open to the poetic, phenomenological, and metaphoric way of experiencing the world.

Avadian, B. (2002). *Finding the Joy in Alzheimer's: Caregivers Share the Joyful Times.* Lancaster, CA: North Star Books.

Barrett, W. (1972). *Time of Need: Forms of Imagination in the Twentieth Century.* Middletown, CT: Wesleyan University Press.

Becker, E. (1973). *The Denial of Death.* New York: The Free Press.

Beaufret, J. (2006). *Dialogue with Heidegger.* Bloomington, IN: Indiana University Press.

Bly, R., Hillman, J., & Meade, M. (Ed.) (1992). *The Rag and Bone Shop of the Heart.* New York: HarperCollins Publishers.

Bohm, D. (1980). *Wholeness and the Implicate Order.* London: Routledge & Kegan Paul.

Boss, M. (1971). *Grundriss der Medizin und der Psychologie.* Bern: Verlag Hans Huber.

Boss, M. (1982). *Psychoanalysis and Daseinsanalysis.* New York: Da Capo Press.

Bryden, C. (2005). *Dancing With Dementia.* Philadephia, PA; Jessica Kingsley Publishers.

Buber, M. (1970). *I and Thou.* New York: Touchstone.

Bugental, E. (2005). *AgeSong: Meditations for Our Later Years.* San Francisco: Elders Academy Press.

Bugental, E. (2007). *Love Fills in the Blanks: Paradoxes of Our Final Years.* San Francisco: Elders Academy Press.

Bugental, J. (1987). *The Art of the Psychotherapist: How to Develop the Skills that Take Psychotherapy Beyond Science.* New York: W. W. Norton & Company.

Bugental, J. (1999). *Psychotherapy Isn't What You Think: Bringing the Psychotherapeutic Engagement into the Living Moment.* Phoenix: Zeig, Tucker & Theisen.

Butler, R. (2002). *Age, Death and Life Review.* In: Doka, K. (Ed.) Living with Grief: Loss in Later Life. New York: Hospice Foundation of America.

Campbell, J. (Ed.) (1955). *The Mysteries: Papers from the Eranos Yearbooks.* Princeton: Princeton University Press.

Capra, F. (1975). *The Tao of Physics.* Boston: Shambhala Publications.

Capra, F. (1984). *The Turning Point: Science, Society, and the Rising Culture.* New York: Bantam.

Castleman, M., Naythous, M., & Gallagher-Thompson, D. (1999). *There's Still a Person There: The Complete Guide to Treating and Coping with Alzheimer's.* New York: Perigee Trade.

Coelho, P. (1997). *Manual of the Warrior of Light.* New York: HarperCollins Publishers.

Coelho, P. (1967). *The Alchemist.* San Francisco: Harper and Row.

Dalai Lama, H.H. (1998). *The Path to Tranquility: Daily Wisdom.* New York: Penguin Group.

Easwaran, E. (Tr.) (1985). *The Bhagavad Gita.* Tomales, CA: Nilgiri Press.

Easwaran, E. (Tr.) (1987). *The Upanishads.* Tomales, CA: Nilgiri Press.

Easwaran, E. (1996). *Seeing With the Eyes of Love.* Tomales, CA: Nilgiri Press.

Easwaran, E. (2000). *With My Love and Blessings: The Teaching Years, 1966-1999 in Photographs & His Own Words.* Tomales, CA: Nilgiri Press.

Feil, N. (2002). *Validation Breakthrough: Simple Techniques for Communicating with People with Alzheimer's Type Dementia.* Baltimore: Health Professions Press.

Feil, N. (2003). *V/F Validation: The Feil Method: How to Help Disoriented Old-Old.* Cleveland: Edward Feil Productions.

Frank, J. (1961). *Persuasion and Healing.* New York: Schocken Books.

Franz, M. (1974). *Shadow and Evil in Fairy Tales.* Boston: Shambhala Publications.

Foucault, M. (1954). *Mental Illness and Psychology.* Berkeley: University of California Press.

Foucault, M. (1965). *Madness and Civilization.* New York: Vintage Books.

Foucault, M. (1972). *The Archaeology of Knowledge and the Discourse on Language.* New York: Pantheon Books.

Fox-Sheinwold, P. (1982). *Too Young to Die.* New York : Bell.

Gadamer, H. (1992). *Truth and Method.* New York: Crossroad Publishing.

Grof, S. & Grof, C. (1980). *Beyond Death: The Gates of Consciousness.* New York: Thames & Hudson.

Gullette, M. (2004). *Aged by Culture.* Chicago: University of Chicago Press.

Hafiz. (2001). *Drunk on the Wine of the Beloved: Poems of Hafiz.* Boston: Shambhala Publications.

Hafiz & Ladinsky, D. (Tr.) (1999). *The Gift: Poems by Hafiz.* New York: Penguin Group.

Hanson, R. (2009). *Buddha's Brain: The Practical Neuroscience of Happiness, Love, and Wisdom.* Oakland, CA: New Harbinger Publications.

Heidegger, M. (1962). *Being and Time.* Malden, MA: Blackwell Publishing.

Heidegger, M. (1966). *Discourse on Thinking.* New York: Harper & Row.

Heidegger, M. (1971). *Poetry, Language, Thought.* New York: Harper & Row.

Heidegger, M. (1975). *Early Greek Thinking.* San Francisco: Harper & Row.

Heidegger, M. (2006). *Mindfulness.* New York: Continuum International Publishing Group.

Helminski, K. (Tr.) (1993). *Love is a Stranger: Selected Lyric Poetry of Jelaluddin Rumi.* Boston: Shambhala.

Hillman, J. (1972). *The Myth of Analysis.* New York: HarperPerennial.

Hillman, J. (Ed.) (1980). *Facing the Gods.* Irving, TX: Spring Publications.

Hillman, J. (1983). *Healing Fiction.* Woodstock, CT: Spring Publications.

Hillman, J. (1989). *A Blue Fire.* New York: HarperCollins Publishers.

Hillman, J. (1997). *The Soul's Code: In Search of Character and Calling.* Warner Books.

Hillman, J. (1999). *The Force of Character: And the Lasting Life.* New York: Ballantine Publishing Group.

Hillman, J. (2004). *The Thought of the Heart and the Soul of the World.* Putnam, CT: Spring Publications.

Hillman, J. & Ventura M. (1993). *We've Had a Hundred Years of Psychotherapy—and the World's Getting Worse.* New York: HarperOne.

Hoblitzelle, O. A. (2010). *Ten Thousand Joys and Ten Thousand Sorrows: A Couple's Journey Through Alzheimer's.* New York, NY: Tarcher.

Hölderlin, F. (2004). *Poems of Friedrich Hölderlin.* San Francisco: Ithuriel's Spear.

Hölderlin, F. (1989). *Hölderlins Werke.* Berlin: Aufbau–Verlag.

Jung, C.G. (1973). *Memories, Dreams, Reflections.* New York: Vintage Books.

Jung, C.G. (1987). *Synchronicity: An Acausal Connecting Principle.* London: Routledge & Kegan Paul.

Kabat-Zinn, J. (1990). *Full Catastrophe Living: Using the Wisdom of Your Body and Mind to Face Stress, Pain, and Illness.* Brooklyn, NY: Delta Publishing.

Kierkegaard, S. (1986). *Fear and Trembling.* New York: Penguin Classics.

Kleinman, A. (1980). *Patients and Healers in the Context of Culture.* Berkeley: University of California Press.

Kleinman, A. (1989). *The Illness Narratives: Suffering, Healing, And The Human Condition.* New York: Basic Books.

Kleinman, A. (1991). *Rethinking Psychiatry: From Cultural Category to Personal Experience.* New York: Free Press.

Krell, D. (1992). *Daimon Life: Heidegger and Life-Philosophy.* Bloomington, IN: Indiana University Press.

Kübler-Ross, E. (1969). *On Death and Dying.* New York: MacMillan Publishing Company.

Levine, P. (1997). *Waking the Tiger: Healing Trauma.* Berkeley: North Atlantic Books.

Luke, H. (1987). *Old Age: Journey into Simplicity.* New York: Parabola Books.

Luke, H. (2001). *The Laughter at the Heart of Things.* New York: Parabola Books.

May, R. (1973). *Man's Search for Himself.* New York: Dell Publishing.

May, R. (1983). *The Discovery of Being: Writings in Existential Psychology.* New York: W. W. Norton & Company.

McBee, L. (2008). *Mindfulness Based Elder Care: A Cam Model for Frail Elders and Their Caregivers.* New York, NY: Springer Publishing Company.

Mindell, Amy (1999). *Alternative to Therapy.* Newport, OR: Zero Publication.

Mindell, Amy (1999). *Coma: A Guide for Friends and Helpers.* Portland: Lao Tse Press.

Mindell, Amy (2003). *Metaskills: The Spiritual Art of Therapy* (2nd edition). Portland: Lao Tse Press.

Mindell, Arnold (1995). *Sitting in the Fire.* Portland: Lao Tse Press.

Mindell, Arnold (2000). *Quantum Mind: The Edge Between Psychology and Physics.* Portland: Lao Tse Press.

Mindell, Arnold (2001). *Dreaming While Awake: Techniques for 24-hours Lucid Dreaming.* Charlottesville: Hampton Roads.

Mindell, Arnold (2001). *The Dreammaker's Apprentice: Using Heightened States of Consciousness to Interpret Dreams.* Charlottesville: Hampton Roads.

Mindell, Arnold (2004). *The Quantum Mind and Healing: How to Listen and Respond to your Body's Symptoms.* Charlottesville: Hampton Roads Publishing Company.

Mindell, Arnold (2007). *Earth-Based Psychology: Path Awareness from the Teachings of Don Juan, Richard Feynman, and Lao Tse.* Portland: Lao Tse Press.

Mindell, Arnold (2010). *Processmind: A User's Guide to Connecting with the Mind of God.* Wheaton, IL: Quest Books.

Molloy, W., & Caldwell, P. (2003). *Alzheimer's Disease.* Toronto: Key Porter Books.

Nin, A. (1967). *The Diary of Anais Nin, Volume 2 (1934-1939).* Orlando: Harcourt Brace & Company.

Oliver, M. (2004). *Why I Wake Early: New Poems by Mary Oliver.* Boston: Beacon Press.

Oliver, M. (2005). *New and Selected Poems: Volume Two.* Boston: Beacon Press.

Pascal, B. (1995). *Pensées.* New York: Penguin Group.

Pearce, N. (2007). *Inside Alzheimer's: How to Hear and Honor Connections with a Person Who Has Dementia.* Taylors, SC; Forrason Press.

Peterson, B. (2004). *Voices of Alzheimer's.* Cambridge: Da Capo Press.

Power, A. (2010). *Dementia Beyond Drugs: Changing the Culture of Care.* Baltimore, MD: Health Professions Press.

Ram Dass (2000). *Still Here: Embracing Aging, Changing and Dying.* New York: Riverhead Books.

Ram Dass (2010). *Be Love Now: The Path of the Heart.* New York: HarperOne.

Richards, T., & Tomandl, S. (2006). *An Alzheimer's Surprise Party: New Sentient Communication Skills and Insights for Understanding and Relating to People with Dementia.* Glenview, IL: Interactive Media.

Rilke, R. (1989). *The Selected Poetry of Rainer Maria Rilke.* New York: Vintage Books.

Rilke, R. (1992). *Letters to a Young Poet.* San Rafael, CA: New World Library.

Rossi, E. (1993). *Psychobiology of Mind-Body Healing: New Concepts of Therapeutic Hypnosis* (2nd edition). New York: W. W. Norton & Company.

Roszak, T. (1998). *America the Wise: The Longevity Revolution and the True Wealth of Nations.* Boston: Houghton Mifflin Company.

Roszak, T. (2009). *The Making of an Elder Culture: Reflections on the Future of America's Most Audacious Generation.* Canada: New Society Publishers.

Rumi, J. (2001). *Selected Poems of Rumi.* Mineola, NY: Dover Publications.

Schneider, K. (2004). *Rediscovery of Awe: Splendor, Mystery and the Fluid Center of Life.* St. Paul: Paragon House.

Schneider, K. (2007). *Existential-Integrative Psychotherapy: Guideposts to the Core of Practice.* New York: Routledge.

Shabahangi, N. R. (2002). *Faces of Aging.* Warsaw: Elders Academy Press.

Shabahangi, N. R. & Szymkiewicz, B. (2006). *Deeper into the Soul.* San Francisco: Elders Academy Press.

Shabahangi, N. R. (Ed.) (2011). *Gems of Wisdom.* Bloomington, IN: iUniverse.

Some, M. (1994). *Of Water and the Spirit: Ritual, Magic, and Initiation in the Life of an African Shaman.* New York: Penguin Compass.

Stafford, W. (1977). *The Way It Is: New and Selected Poems.* St. Paul, MN: Graywolf Press.

Stafford, W. (1986). *You Must Revise Your Life.* Ann Arbor: The University of Michigan Press.

Steinem, G. (2006). *Doing Sixty and Seventy.* San Francisco: Elders Academy Press.

Santorelli, S. (2000). *Heal Thyself: Lessons on Mindfulness in Medicine.* New York, NY: Three Rivers Press.

Suzuki, S. (2002). *Not Always So.* New York: HarperCollins Publishers.

Suzuki, S. (2006). *Zen Mind, Beginner's Mind.* Boston: Shambhala Publications.

Szasz, T. (1970). *The Manufacture of Madness: A Comparative Study of the Inquisition and the Mental Health Movement.* New York: Harper Torchbooks.

Szymkiewicz, B. (2006). *Zranione Stany Swiadomosci [Wounded States of Consciousness].* Warsaw: Eneteia.

Tarrant, J. (1998). *The Light Inside the Dark: Zen, Soul, and the Spiritual Life.* New York: HarperCollins.

Tart, C. (Ed.) (1990). *Altered States of Consciousness.* New York: Harper and Row.

Tart, C. (2001). *Waking Up: Overcoming the Obstacle to Human Potential.* Backinprint.com.

Taylor, R. (2006). *Alzheimer's From the Inside Out.* Baltimore, MD: Health Professions Press.

Terman, S.A. (M. Evans, R. Baker Miller, G. Micco, & T. Mason Pope, eds.)(2009). *Peaceful Transitions: An Ironclad Strategy to Die When and How YOU Want.* Carlsbad, CA: Life Transitions Publications.

Thomas, W.H. (1996). *Life Worth Living: How Someone You Love Can Still Enjoy Life in a Nursing Home - The Eden Alternative in Action.* Acton, MA: Vanderwyk & Burnham.

Thomas, W.H. (2004). *What Are Old People For?: How Elders Will Save the World.* Acton, MA: Vanderwyk & Burnham.

Thomas, W.H. (2006). *In the Arms of Elders: A Parable of Wise Leadership and Community Building.* Acton, MA: VanderWyk & Burnham.

Thurman, H. (1951). *Deep Is the Hunger.* Richmond, IN: Friends United Press.

Thurman, H. (1953). *Meditations of the Heart.* Boston: Beacon Press.

Tischner, J. (1993). *Mylenie Wedug Wartosci [Thinking According to Values].* Krakow: Znak Publishing House.

Twardowski, J. (1994). *Wiersze [Poems].* Bialystok: Lyk Publishing Co.

Voris, E., Fox, P., & Shabahangi, N. (2009). *Conversations with Ed: Why Are We so Afraid of Alzheimer's?* San Francisco: Elders Academy Press.

Watzlawick P., Bavelas J. B., & Jackson D. D. (1967). *Pragmatics of Human Communication: A Study of Interactional Patterns, Pathologies, and Paradoxes.* New York & London: W.W. Norton & Company.

Whitman, W. (1959). *Leaves of Grass.* The First (1855) Edition. New York: Penguin Group.

Wilber, K. (1979). *No Boundary: Eastern and Western Approaches to Personal Growth.* Boston: Shambhala Publications.

Wiseman, R.W. (2003). *The Therapies of Literature.* Warsaw: Elders Academy Press.

Yalom, I. (1980). *Existential Psychotherapy.* New York: Basic Books.

Zeisel, J. (2009). *I'm Still Here: A Breakthrough Approach to Understanding Someone Living with Alzheimer's.* New York: Avery Publishers.

Zeisel, J., & Raia, P. (2000). *Nonpharmacological Treatment for Alzheimer's Disease: A Mind-Brain Approach.* American Journal of Alzheimer's Disease and Other Dementias. 15(6).

Web Resources

Forgetfulness Care – Practice and Learning

www.agesong.com Assisted living management company and developer that believes in the value of aging as an important phase in a human being's development and emphasizes honoring elders as wisdom keepers in our society.

www.agesonginstitute.org AgeSong Institute is dedicated to changing the mainstream view of aging. Rather than viewing aging as something to be avoided, it is seen as an important phenomenon of life.

www.deeperintothesoul.org Interactive website about new approaches to forgetfulness based on symptoms of forgetfulness being meaningful and important for deepening who we are as human beings.

www.pacificinstitute.org Mental health and gerontological training and internship programs which try to help in reconceptualizing the idea of aging to the concept of maturing. Pacific Institute would like to reestablish the role of the elder in our societies.

www.stagebridge.org The nation's first senior theatre company that uses theatre and storytelling to break down stereotypes and create positive attitudes toward aging.

www.sparkoflife.org An innovative program developed in Australia which works with forgetful elders in very respectful terms emphasizing what is present rather than on focusing on what is not.

www.memorybridge.org Memory Bridge creates programs that connect people with Alzheimer's disease and related dementias to family, friends, and other people in their local community.

General Information about Alzheimer's and Dementia

www.alz.co.uk Alzheimer's Disease International (ADI). The umbrella organization of Alzheimer's disease associations around the world.

www.alz.co.uk/help/associations.html Information about Alzheimer's Societies in the world.

www.alz.org Alzheimer's Association in the United States of America. Voluntary health organization dedicated to Alzheimer's care, support and research.

www.alz.org/apps/findus.asp Information about local chapters of Alzheimer's Associations in the United States of America.

www.alzheimers.org.au Alzheimer's Australia. Organization providing support and advocacy for Australians living with dementia.

www.alzheimer.ca Alzheimer's Society of Canada. Organization focused on ways to alleviate the consequences of Alzheimer's and related diseases.

www.alzheimers.org.uk The Alzheimer's Society. Organization that works to improve the quality of life of people affected by dementia in England, Wales and Northern Ireland.

www.alzheimers.org.za Alzheimer's South Africa. Organization that provides support, education, training, and information on matters pertaining to all forms of dementia.

www.alzfdn.org Alzheimer's Foundation of America. Organization interested in providing optimal care and services to individuals confronting dementia, and to their caregivers and families.

www.ahaf.org The American Health Assistance Foundation. Organization that funds research and provides information about Alzheimer's disease.

www.alzbrain.org Resource containing information for caregivers and professionals of persons with dementia, sponsored by the dementia education & training program.

www.pbs.org/theforgetting Site containing information about symptoms and the experiences of Alzheimer's disease, hosted by PBS media enterprise.

www.caregiver.org Family Caregiver Alliance. American organization that addresses the needs of families and friends providing long-term care at home.

www.asaging.org American Society on Aging. Association that works toward improvement of the quality of life of older adults and their families.

Process Oriented Approaches to Symptoms

The following websites include information about process oriented communication with people in altered, remote states of consciousness including dementia and coma. The reader can also find general information about process work and its perspectives on psychological and social issues on these sites.

www.aamindell.net Amy and Arny Mindell. Amy is best known for her development of the metaskill concept in process oriented psychology. Arny developed "process oriented psychology."

www.comacommunication.com Stan Tomandl and Ann Jacob. Ann and Stan do hands on work with people in states of altered consciousness.

www.creativehealing.org Pierre Morin and Kara Wilde. Kara and Pierre are both faculty members of The Process Work Institute of Portland Graduate School who supervise and train process workers.

www.deepdemocracyinstitute.org Deep Democracy Institute. Max and Ellen Schupbach founded Deep Democracy Institute, which provides awareness-based leadership and facilitation trainings. Unlike "classical" democracy, which focuses on majority rule, Deep Democracy suggests that all voices, states of awareness, and frameworks of reality are important.

www.garyreiss.com Gary Reiss. Along with mentor Arny Mindell, Gary is a leading pioneer in developing process oriented coma work: a gentle method for communicating with clients, based on the assumption that all states of consciousness are meaningful and can be worked with.

www.tomrichards.com Tom Richards. Tom uses his awareness abilities to follow people's processes at their deepest sentient levels, encouraging beauty and eldership to come forward even at seemingly impossible times.

www.vfvalidation.org Validation Training Institute. Information about the Validation method, its training and related books.

www.validation-eva.com European Validation Association. An umbrella organization for companies, individuals or foundations that work with the Validation method.

www.stagebridge.org This innovative Senior Theatre company, the first of its kind in the nation, provides a Time*Slips* program that works in a respectful and non-pathological way with forgetful elders.

Eldership Perspectives

Below are listed a few websites that provided some insights for me concerning the concept and practice of Eldership. Far from giving the full spectrum of the sources of inspiration, I would like to present some sites that were subjectively interesting to me and might encourage the reader to do further research.

www.eldership.net Project that aims to foster positive and creative attitudes to the later years of life.

www.easwaran.org This organization offers instruction and guidance in meditation and allied living skills developed by Eknath Easwaran. Their SETU senior retreats are intended for people of retirement age who have fulfilled responsibilities to family and society and are ready to focus on duty to their highest Self.

www.mosaicvoices.org Mosaic formed to create cross-cultural alliances, creative mentoring relationships, and educational projects. Mosaic actively seeks to encourage greater understanding between people with diverse and divergent backgrounds and experiences.

www.worldcouncilofelders.org A nonprofit organization, World Council of Elders, Inc., has been created to facilitate the gathering of the world's indigenous wisdom-keepers, and to help them share their teachings worldwide for the benefit of all peoples.

www.theelders.org Brought together by Nelson Mandela in 2007, The Elders is an independent group of global leaders who offer their collective influence and experience to support peace building, help address major causes of human suffering and promote the shared interests of humanity.

Social Media Resources

www.changingaging.org A platform to counter conventional attitudes towards aging and to provide positive, growth-oriented alternatives for a life worth living.

http://changingaging.org/alpower Songwriter, geriatrician and Certified Eden Alternative® Educator Al Power discusses his ideas about mindful care – all representing fundamentally different approaches and attitudes in assisted living and eldercare.

www.minddeep.blogspot.com Answers to such questions as: What is it really like to practice mindfulness meditation? How can mindfulness practice help with stress, depression, chronic pain, dementia care, end-of-life, and other psychological problems?

About the Author

Nader R. Shabahangi, Ph.D., received his doctorate from Stanford University and is a licensed psychotherapist. His multicultural background has made him an advocate for different marginalized groups of society throughout his adult life. In 1992 he founded the non-profit organization Pacific Institute with the purpose of training psychotherapists in a multicultural, humanistic approach to psychotherapy and to provide affordable therapy services to the many diverse groups living in San Francisco. In 1994, noticing the often-inhumane treatment of elders living in institutions, he developed an innovative Gerontological Wellness Program in order to provide emotional support and mental health care services for elders. In 1997 Nader opened a residential care home for elders in San Francisco, and co-founded AgeSong with the purpose of caring more holistically for elders. AgeSong now manages multiple communities in the San Francisco Bay Area.

Nader extends this perspective with the public through workshops that emphasize aging as a deepening growth process, rather than viewing aging as decline. He is also passionate about understanding forgetfulness, labeled as 'dementia,' as a different state of awareness, and not as a disease.

Elders Academy Press

Elders Academy Press is the publishing house of Pacific Insitute, a non-profit, public service organization, and its elder care program AgeSong Institute.

www.pacificinstitute.org | www.agesonginstitute.org

Elders Academy Press would like to help in developing a vision of a contemporary Elder, a person (or role) we are longing for in our turbulent times – someone who is able to embrace our differences, hopes, dreams and failures. We would like to search for a clearer understanding of what this Elder might be by promoting ideas and values such as:

- Learning to listen to the voices from within and outside ourselves
- Being open to not-knowing and to the mysterious quality of life
- Responding consciously to the world as it is, not as it should be
- Making room for wisdom in our lives by going deeper into experiences
- Trying to understand the language of symptoms as guides
- Allowing space for questioning mainstream ideas and ideals
- Changing patterns of automatic and reactive behaviors

This questioning encompasses also the desire for understanding our meaning and purpose, for looking at life from the different viewpoints and attitudes given by our many cultural, intellectual and spiritual traditions.

Deeper into the Soul: Beyond Dementia and Alzheimer's Towards Forgetfulness Care

by Nader Robert Shabahangi, Ph.D. & Bogna Szymkiewicz, Ph.D.

In *Deeper into the Soul: Beyond Dementia and Alzheimer's Towards Forgetfulness Care*, the authors invite us to shift our attitude toward dementia, or Forgetfulness, as they call it. The goal is to develop a perspective which includes the basic ingredients of openness, curiosity and acceptance.

Deeper into the Soul reminds us that each stage of forgetfulness is a meaningful part of the life journey, during which people experience important emotional and spiritual experiences. Rather than simply a disease, forgetfulness has purpose and meaning; rather than simply being in need of our care, people with forgetfulness can teach us about life and living.

This book is a practical guide for people who work and live with relatives or residents with symptoms of forgetfulness. The authors ask the basic existential questions:

- What are the possible meanings of forgetfulness?
- Is there purpose for both caregiver and the one experiencing forgetfulness?

$13.95, plus tax and shipping

Order online at pacificinstitute.org, or call 415-431-8143

Elders Academy Press
432 Ivy St. • San Francisco, CA 94102

Conversations with Ed
Waiting for Forgetfulness: Why are We So Afraid of Alzheimer's Disease?

by Ed Voris, Nader Shabahangi, and Patrick Fox, in collaboration with Sharon Mercer

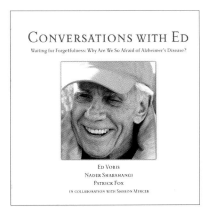

How can we not be afraid of Alzheimer's Disease? How can we not dread aging? By posing these questions we are invited to alternate ways of seeing Alzheimer's disease as well as aging. *Conversations with Ed* wants to create a positive cultural space for people with forgetfulness, for those who accompany them on their journey and for those who fear being afflicted with it.

$25.50, plus tax and shipping

Doing Sixty and Seventy
by Gloria Steinem

Gloria Steinem became a spokesperson for issues about aging on the occasion of her fortieth birthday: "This is what forty looks like." In her inspiring book, *Doing Sixty and Seventy*, Steinem shares her views on age stereotyping, unexpected liberation and the ways women become more radical as they age.

$19.95, plus tax and shipping

Order online at pacificinstitute.org, or call 415-431-8143

Elders Academy Press
432 Ivy St. • San Francisco, CA 94102

Love Fills In The Blanks: Paradoxes of Our Later Years

by Elizabeth Bugental, Ph.D.

Love Fills In the Blanks is an insightful, heart-opening book that examines paradoxes of aging.

This book suggests that the right conditions for seeing and embracing the exquisite beauty that life offers us while at the same time experiencing difficulties that life presents us, are all present once we approach old age consciously—although at times it is difficult to stay aware of the possible hidden in the seemingly impossible.

$19.95, plus tax and shipping

AgeSong: Meditations for Our Later Years

by Elizabeth Bugental

Growing old is not an option. But how we age is a choice. At least we like to think so. *AgeSong* gives us a pleasurable nudge and a little inspiration to take charge of our aging. Now we're old enough and maybe even wise enough to decide how we'd like to live before we die. Maybe we can even choose to do it in style.

$20.00, plus tax and shipping

Order online at pacificinstitute.org, or call 415-431-8143

Elders Academy Press
432 Ivy St. • San Francisco, CA 94102

Rhoda: Her First Ninety Years: A Memoir

By Rhoda Curtis

Six careers. Three husbands. Many lovers. Rhoda's memoir covers nine decades of a life exuberantly lived. Born in Chicago in the Year of the Horse, 1918, she lived and worked through several eras: the late 1920s, the depression years, the years of World War Two, and the postwar period in San Francisco in the Fifties and Sixties; Berkeley and the world in the Seventies, Eighties, Nineties, and the Ought years. Rhoda's stories as a risk-taker will resonate with anyone who has swum against the current.

$20.00, plus tax and shipping

After Ninety, What

By Rhoda Curtis

Where do I go from here? What do I want to do next? Those were the questions that plagued Rhoda when she finished her first book, *Rhoda: Her First Ninety Years*. In the epilogue of the first book, she wrote: "The book is finished, but I'm not." Rhoda needed to reexamine different phases of her life in an attempt to connect its many threads.

$15.00 plus tax and shipping

Order online at pacificinstitute.org, or call 415-431-8143

 Elders Academy Press
432 Ivy St. • San Francisco, CA 94102

Caregiving from the Heart: Tales of Inspiration

by Roberta Cole and Riki Intner

In *Caregiving from the Heart: Tales of Inspiration,* the readers are taken on the life-altering odyssey of caring. At a time in our history when our population is living longer and longer, caregiving has become a national health issue as well as one of the greatest human challenges. The stories in this book cover moments large and small and address elder issues of pressing concern – from painful role reversal, driving, safety and depression, to loss of mobility and even to a last-chance romance.

$19.95, plus tax and shipping

The Therapies of Literature

by Richard W. Wiseman

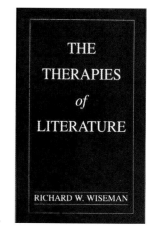

The Therapies of Literature are richer and more human than anything we have yet called psychology. Using names of schools of psychology, Jungian, Bio-energetic, Existential, merely gives a place to start. How many fictions are about human loneliness, human courage? What else does literature have to offer than many guises of one life? This is a deep book written by a true elder.

$13.95, plus tax and shipping

Order online at pacificinstitute.org, or call 415-431-8143

Elders Academy Press
432 Ivy St. • San Francisco, CA 94102

Faces of Aging

by Nader Shabahangi

Faces of Aging is a collection of essays and photographic images that address the challenge of aging in a society that is not sympathetic to older people. The result of this negativity deprives us all from interaction with the last phases of life.

Older people can provide us with experience, knowledge and affection if we change our attitude toward them and begin to see them as a resource rather than a liability. History and the humanistic tradition have shown us that when respected and valued, older citizens can continue to be creative and can contribute to our collective quality of life.

Faces of Aging is a tribute to elders and is dedicated to removing the veil from the subject of aging. The book invites us to ask how we can remain conscious of the ways in which we impose our own fears of aging, of death, of the changes that invariably occur as we age, onto elders themselves. The writing, photos and poems presented will invite the reader to meet with the many images of aging and look anew for meaning in aging and old age, for the maturity and wisdom the Old Wise Guide, inside of us all, offers us.

$19.95, plus tax and shipping

Order online at pacificinstitute.org, or call 415-431-8143

Elders Academy Press
432 Ivy St. • San Francisco, CA 94102

Those who know do not speak;
Those who speak do not know.
Stop up the openings,
Close down the doors,
Rub off the sharp edges.
Unravel all confusion.
Harmonize the light,
Give up contention:
This is called finding the unity of life.

When love and hatred cannot affect you,
Profit and loss cannot touch you,
Praise and blame cannot ruffle you,
You are honored by all the world.

—Lao Tzu
Tao Te Ching